The Widow's Oil

The Guidebook for the Young Widow

Syri A. Harris-Wilson

'78-37476-5 (paperback)

)ited States of America

The Widow's Oil

The Guidebook for the Young Widow

Syri A. Harris-Wilson

Dedication

This book is dedicated to our memories. Life tells us that a person is kept alive by the memories others have of them. Here's to those memories...the good ones, the great ones, the bad ones, the funny ones, the traumatic ones, the sexy ones, the private ones, the cherished ones...

May our loved ones live on because these memories are forever in our hearts.

Thank you for the memories, my Walt, from kindergarten and beyond. I hate that I have acquired the knowledge I have to make this book possible. Yet at the same time, I am glad that I am able to share the knowledge and inspire others who have been, are, and/or will be in my situation. Love you FOREVER!

"Love is how you stay alive, even after you are gone".

~Mitch Albom~

Acknowledgements

This is the part where I honor those very special people who made this book a reality. THANK YOU!!

- God - Because He is everything that you will ever need in ANY situation and the answer to ALL questions you may ever have. Get to know Him if you don't. Come back to Him if you have strayed away.

- My husband Carlin - for helping me to see the reward in striving for Godly excellence in everything that we do. Thank you for your example, elephant.

- My mom - for always being present with love as well as sharing her gift of writing.

- My 6 sons who have all inspired me in many different ways: Christian for his tenacity (follower of Christ), Walter for his meekness, kind heart, and character most like Big Walt (commander for Christ), Caleb for his faithfulness in all things (devotion to Christ), Patrick for his determination and integral, unwavering character (nobleman for Christ), Robert for being resolute in his continued pursuit of greatness (determined for Christ), and James for his wisdom and tenacious ability to access, question, uproot and eradicate old, outdated systems and ways of doing things (supplanter for Christ).

- My Daughter-in-loves India and Victoria and grandchildren Mariyon, SaVanna, and Langston.

- The National Fallen Firefighter Association - for being the support none of us wanted, but we all needed.

- Siobhan and BeFree Inner Circle Community - for the sisterhood, support, accountability, resources, connections, and friendships.

- Lynda D. Mallory - for being the one stop shop to help with this entire process.

- My angel Sifikia - for your Godly example of service, friendship, prayers, and your writings.

- ~My best friend Angie - for simply everything

Table of Contents

Chapter 1

Why I Wrote This Book?

"You are too young to be a widow"...is what I heard more times than you can ever imagine. I would just blankly stare at people and give a half smile. Inwardly, I would be saying, "Oh yea? Well apparently not, cause here I am!" I was 36 years old...

When going through things or faced with something that is unfamiliar, I like to gain insight from those that have had similar experiences. I do this by having conversations with those people and/or by reading books or articles that they may have written. I wrote this book because I was not able to find what I was looking for at the time. What is it that I was looking for you ask? Anything....everything...any little piece of comfort, inspiration, wisdom, direction that would ease my pain in some way and help me to identify my next steps.

I had so many questions. I didn't know where to turn. What I did find was information and some resources for widows that were much older and it was very general. Most of the information did not apply to me and my situation. I came to terms with the fact that either the information I was seeking wasn't available or I just didn't know where to look.

I had loads of support from family, close friends, as well as my fire department family. Sometimes they even made decisions for me (that I had to later undo) because they didn't wanna "bother" me and thought it was something that they should handle themselves.

It made me sad to think about all the widows whose spouses were not service professionals (fire, police, military). I single out service professionals because these groups usually have some sort of internal support program or department for families who are left behind, whether it be locally or some sort of national organization. I thought, "If I feel lost and I have all this built in support, where on the earth would these other widows go that don't have the same assistance or support system? Who helps them? How do they get the answers they need? Who handles things for them when they are having a hard time keeping it together?"

This book is the answer to those questions. It touches on some of the topics that I either had to deal with, still deal with, or that came up throughout the years. I attempted to tackle all the major topics. This book will not be a perfect fit for everyone. You may find it best to handle some of these things differently than I did. That is totally fine. What I AM sure about however, is that EVERYONE who reads this book will gain something from it.

So take a deep breath, relax your shoulders, unclench your jaw, drink some water, and keep reading…

Chapter 2

The "How To" of Grief

Whatisgriefexactly? There are vastly different opinions and definitions depending on whom you ask. I am not Webster, so I will not give you the dictionary definition. Instead, I will give you my list of what it is and is not. My hope is that my list will assist you in some way as you are creating a personal definition that suits you.

Grief IS:

- Different for every person.

- Different among certain age groups.
- Different among various ethnicities.
- Different among genders.
- Something that you may/may not feel directly after a loss.
- Something that you should be patient with and let come however it does for you.
- Something that may require you to seek professional assistance. **(Definitely strongly recommend)** Please consider seeking sooner than later if it is interfering with livelihood and daily functioning.
- Whatever you say, it is for you.
- Fluid. The definition and what it looks like for you may be a certain way one day and totally different the next day or even next hour.
- A time where you may say or do things that are outside of "normal" character.
- Something that is normal.

Grief is NOT:

- A straight line with a beginning, middle, and end dates.
- Something that expires. You can live your life and not have any overwhelming feelings for three years and then all of a sudden BOOM! You are sobbing uncontrollably because something triggered you.
- Something that you have to get approval for.
- Something that anyone can go through FOR YOU.

Now that we have an idea of what it is, let's look further. Did you know that the grief process actually affects our physical bodies? Some of the ways that our bodies respond to grief include:

- Difficulty concentrating
- Irritability
- Sadness
- Numbness
- Anger
- Anxiety
- Disorientation
- Extreme exhaustion
- Headaches
- Lowered immune systems
- Common colds/flu
- Insomnia or irregular sleep patterns
- Tension (especially in neck, chest, throat)
- Joint pain
- Muscle weakness
- Clumsiness
- Being susceptible (almost double) to heart attack or stroke

As you can clearly see from the various ways that grief shows up, it is imperative to recognize these changes in our lives (or the lives of loved ones) and prepare ourselves to deal with these issues. This book will give you some of the tools needed to do just that.

Breathe, drink water, and keep reading...

Chapter 3

It is all about you: Why you Should Come First

This is, by far, the most important chapter in this book. Without this, none of the other material matters. This is it! This is golden... SERIOUSLY! It is a reason that flight attendants tell us to put our oxygen mask on first before assisting others, yes...even our children! We cannot properly help anyone else without first grounding and caring for ourselves.

Oftentimes when people think of self-care, they think of bubble baths, candles, and tea. It is much more than that. All of those things can be included, but it is not what it is in its entirety. We need to take a holistic approach and look at the mind, body, and spirit. All three work together. They must all be considered and included and should not be separated. If you neglect one of the areas, all will suffer. There cannot be internal harmony and peace without tending to all three simultaneously.

You may have the question…"How do you get started with thinking about caring for yourself when you don't even feel like getting out of bed?" and, "When you don't even feel like brushing your teeth?" Well, everything starts with the mindset. Whatever you focus on, that is what will manifest in your life. That being said, how do you view your situation? Are you expecting things to be perfect? To be totally balanced? I hate to be the bearer of bad news, but that is not happening!

For something to be balanced, there has to be an even distribution of weight. Everything needs to be the same all across the board…..impossible and unrealistic when we are speaking about life. The sooner you realize this, the better it will be for you and your loved ones. You will not hold yourself or others accountable for this unrealistic goal. Tell me….Do you know of anyone who has everything together all the time? No. Now, don't get me wrong, there are some periods of time when things can flow smoothly in all areas of life. But, it's just that….periods of time. These times come and go. The first step is to realize that. The world sells us this lie. There is no way that everything will be balanced in life. There are too many pieces of the puzzle to juggle.

Being happy does not mean that everything is perfect. It is just that you have decided to see life beyond the imperfections.
~Author unknown

Instead, what we need to strive for is harmony. Harmony is about an ebb and flow. It is a combination of things coming together and those things working out and making things beautiful in the end. Harmony is attainable. You can have peace in the days when all things are not going smoothly simultaneously, knowing that the day will come soon when things are getting better.

Balance looks like: house being spotless, having no issues at work, all kids being well behaved, listening, doing well in school, and all the bills being paid. Alternately, harmony would look like: the house being a mess this week but you have been able to keep kids on track with all assignments. They have a head start for the upcoming week which then gives you extra time to meal prep on the weekend and give more attention to the house next week...harmony...everything working out...This is doable...this is reality...this takes the pressure off of everyone to be perfect and get everything done immediately...harmony.

Now that we have a clear destination (harmony vs balance), let's develop some consistent, beneficial thoughts. These will then lead to behaviors that will lead to healthy habits and the harmony that we desire. Everything starts with a thought. Decisions, actions, habits, everything. We will discuss more on this topic later in this book. For now, just know that our thoughts determine the direction our lives will take.

After the thought, comes the action or behavior. It is our thoughts being played out. We are conscious of our behaviors. We think about them and make a decision to engage or not engage in specific acts. Habits are unconscious. They are repeated behaviors that are done so often that we perform them naturally, automatically, without thought. These are formed by repeated behaviors.

Developing healthy habits will make your life (especially during this difficult time) much easier. It's like you will be on auto pilot in some areas. This is not to say that you will not have to make any decisions, that you will not forget things, or that some decisions won't be difficult. This will however eliminate and/or make some of those decisions easier because it's something that you already have a system in place to handle. This in turn will lighten your load.

In the next chapter, we will look at the mind, body, and spirit to discuss what specific behaviors we can incorporate into our daily lives in each of these areas. These behaviors will in turn become the healthy habits that lead to the harmony we desire.

The last thing that we need to do before that conversation is to distinguish between the mind and the brain. Some use these terms interchangeably but they each have a unique role and purpose. The brain is the central processing unit of the body and plays a key role in translating the content of the mind into complex patterns of nerve cell firing and chemical release. In other words, the brain is the house for the mind.

Did you know that scientists have been able to trace grief to specific areas of the brain? Follow me for a bit and I promise to not get too scientific here. I'm just trying to shed a little bit of light on what you are going through and the reasons behind it. Once we know better, we do better or often times we can deal with things differently when we know the origin and reasoning behind what we are doing.

Dopamine and Serotonin are chemicals found in the brain. These chemicals work together to keep things harmonious. When grief comes along, the levels at which these chemicals are produced changes rapidly. This throws everything out of whack. Grief also affects our limbic system (system of nerves in the brain) and the prefrontal cortex. These areas are responsible for regulating our emotions, our concentration levels, our multitasking ability and our memory function.

No wonder you feel like you are "going crazy!" Going crazy/being insane is defined as "being in a state of mind which prevents normal perception, behavior, or social interaction" well duuuuuuuh!!!! You just lost somebody who was a significant part of your life in one way or another. Yes, when you are grieving it is safe to say that you are temporarily insane. Key word here is "TEMPORARILY."

I believe that the key is to get the chemicals in the brain balanced again so that the "processing unit" can get back online and give all other parts of the body the correct signals. How do we do that? Glad you asked! Answer is: By doing specific things in each of the following areas that supports the altering of the chemicals mentioned.

Does this sound too scientific? Too technical? It's not. I've got you! You WILL get through this (through not over). You WILL survive. You WILL go on! BREATHE…..drink water….keep reading…

Chapter 4

MINDing Your Business

The first area we will look at is the mind. The mind is a set of cognitive faculties, similar to compartments, that contain things like thoughts, feelings, attitudes, beliefs, memories, judgment, language, and imagination. As mentioned previously, each of these faculties are affected when we are grieving. Some of the things that we can do to assist our minds in this process are:

Getting out in nature: Nature is beautiful. Whether you open a window to get fresh air, let the sun hit your face, sit on the porch or in backyard, lay in the grass, sit by a body of water, play in the rain, walk through a forest, build a snowman, go for a walk, or go for a run, the benefits of being in nature are numerous. Studies have shown that being outdoors boosts your energy and immune system. Breathing phytoncides (which are airborne chemicals produced by plants) increases our levels of white blood cells. This in turn helps us fight off infections and diseases, improves mood, improves vision, mitigates pain, provides free aromatherapy, enhances creativity, improves seasonal affective disorder, provides vitamin D, restores focus, and reduces stress.

Therapy: Therapy is defined as the treatment of a mental or psychological disorder by psychological means. Simply put, it is talking with someone who has had specific training to assist and empower you whenever you feel it's necessary. Our thoughts create our feelings. Our feelings create our behaviors. Our behaviors reinforce the feelings that we have. It is a continuous cycle. It can be helpful to talk with someone who can help us sort out the thoughts that we are having. This is especially important when these thoughts are not producing desired feelings and therefore behaviors. There are different types of therapy (cognitive behavioral therapy, family, psychotherapy, etc.). Within each type of therapy, you will find that there are numerous practitioners and each of their techniques will be different. It is important to not become frustrated if one is not a perfect fit. Take your time, try different practitioners. Find the one where you feel safe and empowered.

Yoga: Yoga originated over 5000 years ago. Although everyone does not agree on its place of origin, none will dispute its benefits. These include: flexibility, increased muscle strength and tone, improved respiration, energy, and vitality, balancing metabolism, weight reduction, cardio and circulatory health, improved athletic performance, protection from injury, better posture, and less stress. There are many different styles of yoga. There are many ways to practice yoga and many places where you can practice yoga. Yoga is not a religion but there are some that use it for religious reasons. Others use it simply for physical benefits. The point is, if this is something that you want to explore, go for it. Research the place where you want to practice as well as the instructor. Ask the instructor questions to see if there is anything that will occur that you are unfamiliar and/or uncomfortable with. Explore more than one area and instructor before forming an opinion. Just like therapy, finding "the right" type of yoga, right instructor, and right place to practice (even if it's in your own home) is important.

Slow/deep breathing: Taking a break to focus on your breath can do wonders for your body. Most people do not breathe properly. Think about a baby and how their belly goes in and out with every breath. This is deep, diaphragmatic breathing and how it is supposed to be done. When we breathe in this manner, it helps us to: lower our heart rate and blood pressure, helps you to relax by lowering cortisol (stress hormone) levels, and improves core muscle stability, just to name a few.

Talking to the deceased: This is just one way to keep the connection with your loved one. Some may think it's crazy, but who cares?! Everyone will experience something different when they do this. Some may actually hear messages from their loved one. Others may just feel a sense of calm and relief come upon them as they share and discuss whatever it is that is on their mind. Neither is right or wrong. Just do whatever makes you feel good.

Prayer: I do not think that I have to say much in this area. Prayer is defined as a solemn request for help or expression of thanks. This is where you make your requests known. Simple. This is definitely a time that help is needed from God. Whatever it is that you practice, whatever it is that you believe, prayer is the simple act of connecting and talking to that higher power. The death of a loved one leaves us with some questions that no human can possibly answer. Prayer is how we can ask some of those tough questions.

Meditation/stillness/mindfulness: If prayer is where we ask the questions, meditation/mindfulness is where we sit and listen for the answers. Mindfulness is a form of meditation. During mindfulness practice, you are intensely aware of all five senses, what is going on around you, how you are feeling, and you focus on one thing at a time. There is no judgment placed on anything whatsoever. It is simply being aware, acknowledging, and moving on. Our lives are so busy that we rip and run 100 miles an hour. If we never take the time to "just be", how do you expect to get or recognize the answers for what you have been praying for?

Think about it this way: This can apply if you are a parent or not. Imagine that you have a child. You love your child with all your heart. You want the very best for them. You have the means to get them their hearts desire. You want to protect them from the craziness that the world offers. You want to teach them, honor them, and show them unconditional love. You wait for the opportunity to provide insight and teach them what you know. You wait and wait...

They come to you daily (maybe)...But when they come, they do so for approximately 5 minutes. During these five minutes, they talk

28

to you. No, not talk, they ask you for things. They may start by saying "thank you" for this or that. But literally for 5 minutes, they read off a list of things that they want you to do for them, as if you are a genie or Santa Claus. After the 5 minutes is up, they leave the room. They never give you a chance to respond. You don't get a word in edgewise. They do this for days, months, years.

This is the nature of your entire relationship. They ask, you listen, and you give. When you don't give them what they request, part of the 5 minutes mentioned above, turns into questioning your decision and/or trying to persuade you that your decision was wrong in hopes of getting their way.

Some of our prayer/meditation/spiritual lives can be this way. At times, we can be like that child. God is that parent. We ask, request, tell about problems, and thank God (if we even remember to do that part). Very rarely do we give the opportunity to hear a response. Meditation and stillness is where we get our answers. Our insights. Our Ah Ha's. Our messages. Our support. We need this. Especially during times of grief when our heads and thoughts are spinning around in circles.

Gratitude: No matter what you believe, it is a universal truth that whatever we give to others and put out in the universe, is what will come back to us. Call it karma, call it fate, call it reciprocity. Whatever you call it, it's fact. Be thankful. Having a daily, intentional, gratitude practice is one way to help get our minds away from the negative thoughts. Gratitude helps us to see things through a clearer lens and focus less on things that we do not have in our lives. It does not negate what has happened. It just puts things into perspective and allows us to see the blessings that we DO have. It

29

also attracts and welcomes more of those great things in. A gratefulness practice can be started at any time. One way to start is to set an alarm for a time that is uninterrupted, in which you can recite or write (maybe journal) all the things that you are grateful for that day. It is a great idea to do this while on a daily walk. You get the benefit of exercise, nature, and gratitude.

Recruiting and accepting assistance from others/delegating: We. Can. Not. Do. It. All. We just can't! No matter how strong we think that we are, we cannot. Remember earlier when I said that we are temporarily insane? Well, how can we expect ourselves to handle all of our regular responsibilities when our mind is not optimal? (Let alone new responsibilities and various things that have come into play).

Answer: You can't! Accept the help that people are offering. The abundance of offers are going to decrease as time goes by and circumstances change, so utilize them as they come in now. If assistance is needed in an area where there have been no offers, speak up. People don't know what you need or if you need anything without your voice.

Remember that this is not an all-inclusive list for helping our minds. Take stock in what works for you. Do more of that.

Breathe….take a sip…keep reading…

Chapter 5

Another Terrible Thing to Waste – The Body

If it is our minds that gives directives and runs the show, then it is our bodies that carry out the orders. The body is the vessel that houses our mind and our spirit. Since we only get one body, we have to do our best to take care of it. When I speak of our body, I am speaking about the inside and the outside. It does no good to eat properly and take supplements if you never exercise or groom yourself. On the other hand, it does no good to jog for an hour daily if you come home and reward yourself by eating junk food or having a cigarette. When you make improvements in one area, more than likely you will be motivated to improve in others. Let's start by taking a look at what you can do for the outward body.

Personal Hygiene: Now I will not get into specifics with you because we all know what this category entails. When we are grieving, we just do not have the energy, desire, wherewithal, motivation, or whatever you want to call it to even get out of the bed some days; let alone wash our hair! However, we cannot afford to neglect this area. This is important. If we become neglectful here, it will only lead to more serious issues down the line.

If you don't want to brush your teeth, well, think about how much more energy it will take to go to the dentist to get cavities filled from your lack of doing so. Don't feel like combing your hair? How about a trip to the hairdresser or barber to cut it all off then when it's too matted to comb through? Not interested in taking a shower? How about having to use the topical ointment 3x a day that the dermatologist has had to prescribe because you have had an eczema flare up due to not washing routinely? Which would you rather?

Now I am not saying that you need to prepare and look as if you are going to a black tie affair everyday. Keep it simple during this time of grief. Take stress off yourself. Remember those volunteers that we spoke of? Let them come over and pick out a week's worth of clothing for you (underwear and socks included). I don't care if it's leggings and t-shirts. All you need is something clean and tailored to whatever you have to do for the week. Think about low manipulation hairstyles that will last a while so that you do not have to do much to your hair to look and feel presentable. Repeat weekly until the outside assistance is no longer needed and you are able to do these things on your own.

Exercise: Please don't all jump me at once! I am not saying run out and get in debt to get an expensive gym membership or run to purchase expensive equipment for a home gym (unless: you will utilize it and it will help you, you want to, you are able to afford it, and you have been thinking about this even before the tragedy). When I say exercise, I simply mean MOVE YOUR BODY. Dance, jump, run, skip, skate, go to gym, walk, hop, play kickball, throw the kids or pets up and down, you get the point......Just MOVE CONSISTENTLY for at least 30 minutes DAILY.

Studies show that doing 30 minutes of daily exercise can assist with: Lowering blood pressure and blood sugar, improve your mood, reduce stress, give you a burst of energy, tap into creativity, improve your memory, minimize your risk of stroke, cardiovascular disease, diabetes, metabolic syndrome, muscle strength, endorphin production, just to name a few!! Doesn't this list sound like everything we need during this time?

Massages: Whether you treat yourself to some fancy spa, find a great 2 for 1 deal on Groupon, visit your local massage therapy school, barter with a friend, ask someone for a favor, or put lotion on yourself and self-massage.....get rubbed! Three things happen when you get a massage. 1. Your body thanks you because it is getting attention in areas that are often overlooked. 2. You get circulation going throughout your body, which only improves all functions. 3. You are taking a break from LIFE to focus on yourself and hit the restart. You need and deserve this.

Pampering: This category is <u>subjective</u>. Everyone has a different definition of what it means to be pampered. This could be:

- a long (or at least longer than usual)
- getting a manicure/pedicure
- going to get hair done
- getting a facial
- going solo to treat yourself to a slow walk around Target
- Going to get your favorite tea or coffee
- sitting alone at your favorite spot to daydream or think about nothing at all
- going to your favorite place for a meal
- reading your favorite book

The point is, whatever you can do for yourself that makes YOU feel good, that makes YOU smile, do that. INTENTIONALLY! Set time for it or it will not happen. I mean it! Write in in your planner or add it to your calendar events in your phone. Set an alarm for yourself. Treat it as you would a doctor's appointment or any other very important occurrence. Because it is important. It's the MOST important. I promise you that the activity will boost your spirits. It will give you something to look forward to in the weeks to come.

Sleep: Sleep deprivation is something that most people just "deal with" and do not realize how it affects them. Sleep may seem ever fleeting, especially after a loss. Being deprived of this precious nightly gem can lead to: Memory issues, trouble with thinking and concentrating, mood changes, accidents, weaken your immune system, raise your blood pressure, put you at risk for diabetes, weight gain, lower your sex drive, put you at risk for heart disease, and even poor balance:

Most of us do not get the amount and/or type of sleep that we need. We have all heard that we should get 7- 8 hours of sleep per night. This will vary for people and is actually not as important as the quality of sleep that one receives. 7+ hours of consistent, good quality, sleep is difficult for a lot of us. Parenting duties, extracurricular activities, second jobs, and small children make it even more difficult for this to occur.

When we add grief to the scenario, varied sleep patterns are a common occurrence. Nothing is "normal" during this time. Some people lose sleep while others sleep increases. This is one way that the body is adjusting and trying to recalibrate for all the emotions and changes it is feeling. I recommend reaching out to a professional (primary physician and/or mental health specialist) if your sleep pattern has become so erratic that it prevents you from eating or caring for yourself or dependent loved ones.

If you find that you are not getting enough sleep, here are some things that you may consider to at least improve the quality of sleep that you do receive. These are: sticking to a specific schedule for waking and going to bed, creating a relaxing ritual before bed and wind down, exercise daily, evaluate your mattress and pillow, avoid bright light in evening and get sunlight in morning, avoid dark chocolate, alcohol, cigarettes, and heavy meals at least three hours before bed, avoid tossing/turning in bed. If you cannot sleep, go to another room and do something relaxing (i.e. sit and listen to music, reading, etc.) until you are sleepy, try natural supplements like melatonin and magnesium.

Hobby: Hobbies are good for your mental health, improves your creativity, and reduces stress. What do you like to do? Do you remember? Taking a while to sit with yourself to remember will be beneficial. Write a list. Try one thing on the list at a time. Determine if you still like that particular thing.

If you cannot think of anything, maybe this is the time to begin making the list. That can be exciting! You can start by asking your family members or close friends to name a few things that they like. Then explore and do one of those things. If you liked it, keep it for your list. If not, scratch it off and go to the next item. Sounds like a "common sense" thing, I know. But honestly, we get so tied up with family, work, children, spouses, and daily duties, we can forget what it is we actually enjoy. I know I did.

Eating properly and taking supplements: Just like any machine, our bodies need the proper fuel to function and do what it is naturally supposed to do. It gets its fuel from whatever we put into it and whatever we do to it. You have already heard all the clichés (You are what you eat, etc.) and I am no personal trainer, so I will not bother you with those here. You know what to do. This just serves as a gentle reminder, a little nudge if you will. If you are not convinced, try a little experiment for yourself.

Keep a log. Go one week eating whatever you want to eat. Don't change anything. Eat the way you normally would. Write down times you ate, what you ate, and how you felt one hour after eating/drinking whatever you consumed.

The week that follows (2nd week), do the same thing. The difference is that this week you are a little more mindful of consumption. Ideally, this would be a week of nothing but fruits, veggies, quality cuts of meat (if any), no processed foods. Write down the same things. Write what you ate, the times you ate it, and how you felt one hour afterwards. If this change in diet is too drastic for you and you cannot stick with it, get as close to ideal as possible.

Then the third week, compare the previous two weeks. What happened? Do you see and feel a difference? I am confident that you will.

Our bodies need proper nutrients. They crave it. The older we get, the more we need to be close to what is considered optimal because we naturally lose some of the things that our body creates on its own. Not only do the majority of us not eat what we are supposed to, but when we do eat properly, we do not consume enough of what's needed for our body to work at an optimal level. The other thing that happens is because we are not eating properly on a full time basis, the nutrients from the good food cannot be fully absorbed because of the blockages created by the bad stuff we have been shoving into our mouths for years.

This is where supplements come into play and they fill in the gap for us. Just as an example, it is said that our bodies need approximately 3500-4700 mg of potassium from food on any given day. A stalk of broccoli contains about 371 mg of the potassium needed. Now, I could either eat about 10 stalks of broccoli a day OR I could eat a normal portion, along with some other healthy foods, and then take some supplements that contain the extra potassium and other things that are needed for the day to handle the deficit. Which would you rather? When we give our body what it needs, it will respond appropriately and give us strength to heal and deal with our emotions, decisions, and grief. Everything is connected.

Drinking enough water: This section could easily apply elsewhere in this book and it is so important that it deserves its own spot. When do you drink water? How often do you drink water? How much do you drink at one time? Throughout the day? Water intake is so important. At least 60% (over two-thirds) of our body is made of water. That means it needs at least this much in order to operate properly. When the body loses any amount (sweat, urine, etc.), it needs to replenish it somehow. When the body is not replenished, the result is dehydration.

Dehydration is defined as, "a harmful reduction in the amount of water in the body." Harmful is the key word here. People often just drink water when they are thirsty. This is a mistake. By the time you are thirsty, it is too late. You are already dehydrated. This upsets the balance of minerals in your body. This in turn affects the way the body functions...in ALL areas.

When you are dehydrated you can get: headaches, dizziness, sleepiness, decreased urination, decreased skin elasticity, dry mouth/bad breath, low blood pressure, just to name a few. On the other hand, you can prevent dehydration by drinking plenty of water. If cleared by a medical professional to do so, you can start with drinking 1/2 your body weight-in ounces of water. If you weigh 200 pounds, try drinking 100 ounces of water daily. Other ways to avoid dehydration are: eating foods with high amounts of water (fruits and vegetables), avoiding or limiting caffeine intake (coffee, tea, soft drinks), and avoiding or limiting alcoholic beverages.

Some of the advantages of staying hydrated are: keeps hunger at bay and assist with overeating (sometimes when we feel that we are hungry, we are simply thirsty), increases energy and brain function, helps joints and muscles function correctly, cleanses your body, promotes cardiovascular health, and maximizes physical performance. Water is LIFE!

Baths/Sauna: Baths are as old as time. They have been used as medicinal and as a form of beauty for centuries. We can add things to baths that serve different purposes (i.e. Epsom salt, flowers, milk, apple cider vinegar, oatmeal, herbs, essential oils). Baths can elevate our mood, improve circulation, relax us, improve quality of sleep, balance hormones, relieve muscle pain, burn calories, improve skin, and lower blood pressure.

Saunas are something that have been used for centuries as well. There are four different types of saunas. These are Finnish, dry, steam (or Turkish), and infrared. Although each have their own unique properties, they have been proven to detoxify the body, relieve stress, and enhance your mood, increase circulation, and lower inflammation. Inhale. Exhale. Drink your water. Keep reading…

Chapter 6

You've Got Soul. . .and Spirit Too

These terms are often used interchangeably but are not the same thing. The purpose of the spirit is to handle spiritual things. We are spiritual beings. We have a soul, we live in a body, but we are spirits. When a person becomes a Christian and accepts God as the head of their life, they are given the gift of the Holy Spirit to lead and direct them in all areas and all matters from that point forth.

The soul on the other hand is what is inside. It contains our mind, emotions, feelings, and will. This book is not solely for Christians. However, I needed to lay that foundation so that as you continue to read, you will know that I am speaking from the definitions that I have referred to above.

In order to "make your soul sing", as the popular saying goes, you have to first have a clear understanding about what the soul is and what it contains. If it contains our thoughts and emotions, let's examine our thoughts about a particular matter. What are the thoughts that you have related to the loss of your loved one? What emotions come to the surface when these thoughts arise?

Once we have a clearer understanding of the components of the soul, we can take a step further and begin to identify the things that make us happy (our soul sing). What do you like? What do you dislike? These sound like simple questions but so often we are caught up in our other roles (wife, mother, church member, and employee) that we forget ourselves. We can lose sight of what makes our insides jump for joy.

When a loved one dies, there are often feelings of extreme overwhelm. How can we go on? How can we survive? Part of the reason for this feeling of overwhelm is because we have been so preoccupied with particular roles (along with its duties and responsibilities) that we lose sight of one of the most important relationships, the one with ourselves. We do not remember ourselves outside of that person. Who am I? Who was I before I was married/in that relationship? What did I like to do? Whom did I hang around? These can be difficult questions to answer.

Let's do an exercise. After you have answered the questions above, close your eyes and visualize that person you described. What did they look like? Where did they live? What did they drive? How did they dress? Did you like this person? Were you happy? Were you content? Are there some things that you can glean from that person and bring into the present? What are some of the steps needed to get you closer to that?

Maybe your answer was NO and you did not like anything about that person, which is fine. Visualizing that person and the things that you did not like, will give you a foundation to build upon. You can begin by visualizing the exact opposite of those things that you identified as unfavorable.

Change can be difficult. Some changes are easier than others. When dealing with any sort of changes/ transitions, other people's opinions (or perceived opinions) can feed our insecurities and hold us back from taking those steps toward the person we truly want to be. *"Insecurity is a direct threat to our destiny"* ~Pastor Sarah Jakes Roberts~ We either feed the insecurities and stay stagnant or move forward (even with the insecurities) and move closer to our destiny. Are you one that is overly concerned and maybe even consumed with the opinion of others? Don't be. Simply, do not be concerned! People will always have something to say and that's fine. They are respectfully entitled to their opinion and, it is just that, their opinion. You don't have to own it, you don't have to do anything with it whatsoever. It is not your responsibility to do so. Easier said than done, I know. Believe me, the sooner you can tap into this ideology, the better you will feel as you are trying to pick up the pieces of your life.

After you complete the visualization exercise, let's take a smaller step. I challenge you to get a piece of paper and something to write with and write a list of 10 things that make you smile and light you up inside. Make revisions and add items and/or delete items as needed. Do not over think it. Do not second guess yourself. No judgment. You can burn the list when you finish it if you want. Only rule is to be honest with yourself.

Identifying your likes and dislikes is one of the first steps in knowing or remembering who you are. Now that you have done that, know the greatest gift you can give to yourself and to others around you at this time is to stay true to the list you made for yourself. Always be yourself, the authentic you.

If this is who you are, doing things outside of those that are on your list, will not make you happy and is ultimately a waste of time. You will go through the motions and things may get done, but you may end up feeling like a robot. Your soul will not fully rest and be at peace until it reaches happiness. You will go through the same cycles, be involved with the same people, and end up in the same dissatisfied place until you do something different. The true happiness that I mention will only come when you are doing the things you care about and surrounding yourself with people who are supportive, make your heart sing, and that you love.

Let me give you an example. Imagine that you are the neighborhood watch club president. This role is something that you just "fell into" because you had been in the neighborhood for a while and you started attending meetings to discuss a couple things that you wanted to see changed. You were vocal in the meetings and shared your ideas, which others thought were wonderful. You gained the support of many people and committees were formed, you joined and completed the tasks that needed to be done. Elections came up and you were nominated. Everyone was excited and convinced you that you would be great because of all the progress that had been made thus far. You accepted the nomination and won unanimously.

But, you don't enjoy the responsibilities. Every time something has to be done for the group, you dread it. It pulls you away from what you really want to be doing and consumes your time. You are grouchy and short tempered with those around you as you prepare to complete your tasks and are not your best or nicest to the participants when you are in the group. STOP IT!!! Why are you doing the thing that is not mandatory and taking time from things that you could be doing that you love and bring you joy? Focus on things that you love. Most people spend their lifetime trying to discover their "purpose". Well, chances are that the "purpose" that people are so obsessed with finding, is likely tied to what they love and would be doing for free.

Discover and rediscover what REALLY makes you happy. Forget others' opinions of you, take steps to incorporate more of those things in your life, as well as taking steps to eliminate the things that do not align with the direction you are proceeding. Consider the following on your quest to make your soul sing:

Church or religious group/organizations: No matter your spiritual beliefs, people have an innate desire to belong to something. We want to be around individuals and/or groups that share common interests, beliefs, and ways of doing things. Most of these groups have some sort of instructions, directives, suggestions,

45

a stance, bylaws, creed, or a mission statement that they live by. Within these, you will find verbiage on how you can be supported during this time.

This is the time to lean on the members of your groups. Reach out to your support system. Since you share common beliefs, they will more than likely know the words and guidance that can bring comfort to your soul and assist in healing your heart.

If you are not part of a particular group, maybe you can talk to a friend or family member that you consider to be supportive or who has desirable character traits. Ask them if they are involved in any groups/organizations that they feel may support you. Make sure that you do your research before joining. It should reflect your beliefs, interests, and address your concerns. This group should bring you comfort and you should be able to find support, solace, and receive encouragement from belonging. Consider bereavement groups in your area. Wherever it is, find your place. You are not alone. You belong.

Develop a regular routine: Consistency can help with an idle as well as an overactive mind. If you are consistent with a similar routine on a daily basis, you won't have to make the decision about what to do next. Things are done and progress is made without you having to use one simple brain cell for figuring it out, and this is a WIN/WIN! This is NOT to say that every single moment must be regulated. You need to give yourself time to breathe, relax, cry, do nothing, walk, and handle unexpected things that may come up. If there is at least a skeleton or outline of the day, this could be of great benefit.

Taking care of your home is one area that may not be a high priority during this time and this is ok. I recommend accepting those offers of help to assist you. You can also develop a simple routine on your own. A Google or YouTube search will give you all the examples that you need. My personal favorite is www.flylady.net.

Laugh: Proverbs 17:22 says, "A merry heart doeth good like a medicine…" No matter your race, religion, ethnicity, or belief system, this is true for everyone! Laughter has been scientifically proven to:

- boost your immune system
- improve cardiac health
- lower your blood pressure
- improve your mood
- reduce stress
- increase endorphins

Make an effort to laugh each day. There are some times where it may not seem as if there is much to even smile about, let alone laugh. I get it. Acknowledge and honor those times when you don't feel like laughing. Afterwards, go back to laugh between the tears.

You can do this by incorporating things like: surrounding yourself with family and friends who can bring a smile to your face, watching a bunch of funny things on social media, pulling up comedy on Netflix, going to the movies to watch the latest funny release, or trying out laugh yoga (yes, it is really a thing) just to name a few. Whatever you do, be intentional about allowing yourself space to laugh. Make time for it and put it in your day.

Thankfulness: The simple act of being grateful can only bring more things into your life for which to be grateful. Read that again. Make gratitude a daily practice by setting a specific time to think about it each day, journal or maybe go on a walk and say out loud the things that you are grateful for in life. Tell people thank you when they do something for you. No matter how bad a situation is, it could always be worse. Don't believe me? Give it a try for a week. Notice the changes in how you feel as well as things that occur in your life.

Family and friends: This may seem like a no-brainer, but often when we lose someone close to us we want to crawl into a shell and isolate ourselves from the world. This temporary isolation from all people and/or specific people may be a necessary step in your healing and there is nothing wrong with that. However, if you are fortunate enough to have people in your corner who are truly genuine, that are truly able to handle some tasks to get them off your plate or just provide emotional support, lean on them! We often underestimate how good it feels and the benefits being around loved ones can provide. The words of encouragement, the hugs, the support in little tasks, are all priceless.

Yoga: As mentioned previously, there are many different types of yoga. They range from full aerobic, where you can work up a sweat ,to holding poses for a longer time and focusing on your breath to increase flexibility. Yoga is not about getting into pretzel like positions and chanting "oooooommmmmmmm" with your eyes closed. Instead, yoga is a discipline, which incorporates various physical, mental, and spiritual practices. The word itself is derived from Sanskrit root "Yuj" which simply means "union, to join, or yoke."

If you choose this avenue as something that you want to consider, you will need to find which type works for you. Not all yoga routines are created equal.

I want you to notice that the suggestions that I gave for each section may overlap. As I mentioned previously, EVERYTHING is connected. When we do something to care for (or neglect) one area, it affects the other.

Did your jaw clench up again? Take Notice. Unclench. Brows furrowed? Take Notice. Unfurrow. Get more tissue, drink your water, take another deep breath, keep reading...

Chapter 7

Expect Nothing, Forgive Everything

F orgiveness and grace are words that you will need to learn and use often during this period. Pain, especially emotional, is something that most try to avoid. It makes us feel uncomfortable. Most, but not all, people have the desire to say and do the right things. They want to say or do something to assist with the pain that we are experiencing (or at least not add to that pain). The issue is that oftentimes, the best words are not always presented. People are so focused on relieving the discomfort (ours and theirs) that they quickly mimic what they have heard others say and what they think is the right response. They want to fill the void of silence. This occurs often to the detriment of how the words may be received by the other party.

Think about how often we ask others the very simple question, "How are you?" As a widow, can you remember being asked that question when you were in the midst of one of "those days" where nothing was going right? You know the type of day where you are like that pressure cooker in your kitchen and you just can't. take. one. more. thing?! On those days, did you ever imagine yourself as a samurai where you slowly pulled your very sharp sword out from your side and then you sliced their body in half? No?!! Was that only me? Fine then. Moving on....LOL

Let's look at this from the viewpoint of the one asking the question. If they were completely honest about what they wanted to say, it would probably be something like: "Tell me how you are if you are faring well and dealing with things in a relatively calm manner. If you are however freaking out, crying uncontrollably, losing control of your mental faculties, not eating, and everything seems to be falling apart, please keep that to yourself because I wouldn't know what to do with that information."

Taking a moment to pause and put ourselves in the other person's shoes goes a long way. It is the first step in allowing for grace for others. It eliminates the need to walk around with a chip on your shoulders all day because people are not responding a certain way, saying the things we think they should say, or doing what we feel they should do. We would find ourselves apologizing or regretting what we say, a lot less. This probably will not happen because it would require that each person was honest about their feelings and intentions and put forth that effort. The reality is that some people

Syri A. Harris-Wilson

are just not willing or able to do so. However, we as widows can do our part. We can use our unique insight and lead by example in the questions and comments that we make to others.

Another thing that we can do for ourselves and to enlighten others about these sorts of interactions, is to refuse to give the robotic answer: "I'm fine" or "ok" to these questions. We do not have to unload on each person, but we have the right to feel our feelings and express them when we want, how we want, especially after a great loss. You might say something like: "I am not doing too well and if I told you all the details, it would probably stress us both out. I do not even want to discuss it all. So just keep me in your prayers and positive thoughts." This type of response provides self-validation as well as provides an opportunity for learning and growth for others.

Another way that people may deal with this emotional discomfort is by extending a helping hand or promising to do so. People make all types of promises when they see someone hurting. Most do so without hesitation and without considering whether it is something they really are interested in completing, willing to do, or if it conflicts with anything in their own personal lives. Again, it is my belief that the majority of these people have good intentions. I mean, what type of monster would tell someone who recently lost their spouse that they are going to help do something with absolutely no intentions of doing said thing? My advice: Do not hold them to the things they say. Hear it. Be appreciative. If it happens, it happens. If it doesn't, it doesn't. PERIOD.

If you adopt the attitude of gratefulness and appreciate anything extra that others do for you, this will cause you less frustration when

53

those that made promises to do something, don't hold up to what they said. Do not try to figure out the reason they didn't do what they said they were going to do. Don't guilt them into completing the tasks. Those that are meant to assist you, will. Those that are able to be present, will. Maybe they were called into work that day, maybe they had a family emergency, maybe they started doing the thing that they promised for you, it triggered something in them, and they had an emotional breakdown and just couldn't complete the task. Whatever the reason, fact is, they were not obligated to do anything. This is YOUR life. This is a situation that happened to YOU, not them. No matter how unfair it may seem, you are the one that lost your partner. Be grateful for anything that others offer and forgive them when they don't show up or follow through.

All that being said, this is not to say that you just blindly and frivolously trust everyone and allow them to put you in difficult situations repeatedly. For instance, if someone offers to pick the children up from school for a month and they forget a couple times the first week, it would be silly to let them continue with the responsibility. This puts you in a bind and puts extra burdens on you; more than you already have. What I would suggest in a situation like this, is to have a conversation with them, relieve them of the responsibilities, and find someone else reliable until you are able to assume the responsibility again. You may say something like, "I really appreciate the way you stepped in and offered to pick my kids up from school. However, it doesn't seem to be working. I am going to arrange to have them picked up. There are many other things that I am going to need assistance with. I will call you as they arise." This way you are in complete control and you can decide whether to assign them another duty or nothing at all.

Another lesson that I had to learn is to forgive and not take it personal when left out of events. Remember when we talked about people not liking to face pain? Well, you're going to have to realize that your sheer presence can make people uncomfortable and remind them of the deceased. It is sheer reality. It's not your fault and not their fault either.

You will have some people who are able to overcome this fact and invitations will continue. But, you will also have some who don't know what to do for these dinner parties, functions, celebrations or milestones and choose to deal with the anxiety by not extending the invitation. Do not take this personally! Don't hate them for it. Everybody handles things differently. Just as you have a right to refuse an invitation, a phone call, and a visit when you are not up to it, they have the same right. Wouldn't you rather not receive an invitation than receive one and things are awkward and uncomfortable the entire time that you are present? Forgive them. Do not hold them to it and don't give passive/aggressive hints. The ones that meant it, are able to handle it, and are supposed to be there, will be. Express your gratitude to all that offer and see what happens.

On the other hand, if there are some people who extend invitations or offerings of assistance and you do not get a good vibe from them, it's ok to say NO! Trust your instincts! Everyone does not have good intentions. These instincts are your protection and there for a reason. Politely thank them for the offer and explain that you just need time to be alone or time with your immediate family and you will contact them if needed. This puts the ball in your court.

You are in control. You have this... BREATHE...KEEP GOING.....KEEP READING...

Chapter 8

This or That?

When my husband passed away, there were numerous decisions to make. I was grieving, parenting, running a household, and trying my best to keep it together. Who wanted to deal with a load of decisions? Not me! Nonetheless, the decisions just sat there, like stubborn little children, waiting for me to finish my temper tantrum and address them.

Decisions are one of those things that we take for granted. They are so ingrained in our daily lives that most of us tend to make them without much thought. These include simple things like: which way to turn at an intersection, what's for dinner, how to respond to a specific person or situation, or what outfit to wear on any given day, etc.

Most of us are able to make these decisions without a second thought. Ideally, they are made rationally, quickly, and according to how we perceive a situation. The problem is when you are grieving you are not always rational. Your brain is foggy. Let's discuss the different types of decisions and what can be done with each type.

Major Decisions

These types of decisions are those that are completely life altering. Examples of these are: change of residence, changing jobs, change in school, selling personal belongings, etc. These types of decisions should be avoided directly after a loss if at all possible. Remember we mentioned that as you are grieving, you can be irrational and temporarily insane? Why would you make a major decision during this time? Why take a chance with making the one that you will not be happy with in the future? I recommend putting off these types of decisions for at least one year after a loss. Although we are all different and there is no set time that this fog lifts, one year provides enough time for the ebb and flow of thoughts and emotions to have gone through at least one cycle of the highs and lows and even out a bit.

After this time, you may find that things are a little clearer and easier to handle. There is nothing worse than making a hasty major decision. Imagine this example: You decide to sell your home and move to another city with your children away from your family and friends. You wake up one day and realize that you are alone and away from all your support.

58

Another less drastic example is deciding to get rid of all your deceased loved ones clothing. You think this is a good idea because of the emotions that you feel when you see them. Then three months down the line, you or your children wish you had just one piece of clothing to remind you of your loved one. The clothes are gone and never coming back. There is nothing you can do to get them back. Take your time with these types of decisions. There is no rush.

SEPARATING OTHER DECISIONS

One way to make your choices a little easier is to write a list of all decisions that must be made along with deadlines for each. Go over this list numerous times to ensure that it is all-inclusive. Then separate the list into three categories: those decisions that can be delegated, those decisions that must be made immediately (within three months), and those that can be made later (three or more months). Mark the deadlines on your calendar so that you will not forget them. This list should also be reviewed and edited at least monthly. Remove old things that have been completed, and add new things as they come up.

DECISIONS THAT CAN BE DELEGATED

No. You cannot do it all! Well, you probably can, but why attempt to at this time when you have others offering to help? You just lost someone extremely important to you. There will be a lifetime of decisions you will have to make for yourself and others. Let capable and trustworthy people who have your best interest at heart help you. You will burn out and/or crack up trying to do it all.

59

Besides, most of these offers of help will greatly decrease or subside all together after a short while. Most people mean well but after a couple weeks/months, most will go back to their lives and get busy with their own decisions, duties, etc. You may actually want some assistance later when there is no one around. Get it while the getting is good. One example of a decision that can be put into this category is: What's for dinner? Allow someone to create a weekly meal plan based on things that you and your family like to eat and then write out a grocery list. Even allow them to shop if they offer.

DECISIONS THAT MUST BE MADE IMMEDIATELY

There are some things that you may not be able to put off and require your immediate attention. My recommendation for these things are:

- Double/triple check to determine whether these are in the correct category. Ask yourself what will happen if this decision is delayed or not made at all. If after this, you determine that it must be made, then proceed.

- For simple yes or no decisions, make a list of pros and cons for deciding one way or the other. Pros should outweigh the cons. Decide accordingly.

- If you have someone that you can trust, feel confident in their decision-making skills, and feel comfortable with them knowing your business, and run the decision by them as a second opinion. Give them the reasons for the decision and listen to their input. Note that input does NOT mean that you have to change your decision if you do not agree with them. Remember that YOU are the expert of your life.

- Have confidence in your decision. Cross that one off the list and move forward with the next one. We often guess, second guess, triple guess our decisions. Do not do this to yourself. Especially right now in your time of healing. Allow yourself some grace and room to be imperfect. So many other things need your energy and focus. It's ok! Worst-case scenario is that you have made a decision that you wish were different. You may have chosen A instead of B. You will have to deal with those consequences. Guess what? There is a lesson in ALL things. You were supposed to choose the exact way that you did. Take pride in that and know that you will learn from the outcome no matter which way you choose.

DECISIONS THAT CAN BE PUT OFF UNTIL LATER (THREE MONTHS OR MORE)

These things do not require your immediate attention. Nobody else can make these types of decisions for you, but it is nothing that you have to handle at this moment. An example of something that may fit this category is whether to attend a family reunion that is eight months away. You may need to decide this type of thing soon so that you can look into flight costs, reserve a room, etc. but you will not miss the mark if you put this decision off for the moment to make room for others that are more pressing right now.

I recommend that you review and revise this list at least weekly. Take off things that you have completed. Add new things to the proper category as they arise. Review deadlines that you have assigned to ensure they have not changed.

It is worth mentioning that we do not often give ourselves enough credit. We do things that we consider "normal" and do not realize the effort that it takes to complete these tasks. Everything accomplished during this time is a big deal! One way that would help keep this into perspective is to keep the list of things that you have completed. Review your list when you feel like you are stagnant and not being productive.

Breathe…drink water…keep reading…

Chapter 9

Finances

L osing your significant other causes concern in many different areas. Among them is money, especially if the significant other was the sole provider, or if their income was more than half of the household income. There can be a whirlwind of thoughts. How will we make it? Will I have to move away from my home? How will we eat? What about my future? All of these are great questions and all need to be answered. But, not all at the same time.

As explained earlier, this is your life and it has been rocked to the core. Everything does not have to be figured out immediately. Prioritize. What is most pressing at this very moment? Does your budget need adjusting? Do you even have a budget to adjust? Are you working full time but may need to make a change due to childcare/school issues? Is your landlord/mortgage company contacting you for payment that you do not have? PAUSE. BREATHE. KEEP READING. Assessment time…

Take a piece of paper and list all questions that arise in your head as it relates to money and income. All of them. When this list is complete, look over all the questions to see if you have missed anything. Done? Ok now we start from ground zero. Where are you TODAY? Which of these questions require an immediate answer? What needs your attention right this very second?

Write those things down separately. Next to each item, write down the actions step needed to get the answer. For example, if you have no idea when your current bills are due because you did not pay the bills, the action step that is needed is to contact all utility companies and creditors to determine due dates and payment amounts. Do you need to make additional phone calls? Do you need to find a professional in a specific area? Do you need to do some calculations to figure things out? Knowing where you are starting is the key to moving forward with any plan.

If you are working, the first thing to do is to contact your employer's human resources department to discover all options that you have so that you can decide which to choose. How much time can you take off to sort things out? Is this time paid or unpaid? Which fits your immediate needs? Ideally, it would be the one that offers time off with income that meets the needs of your family.

Next thing to do is sort and assess your bills. If you don't know what bills you have (maybe your loved one took care of all that) or you don't know the exact amounts owed for various things, that is your first step. Take stock and assess. On a sheet of paper, write down everything that you spend money on in a month as well as the approximate amounts that you spend. If thinking about a month is too much, scale back, think about a week, and multiply those numbers by 4 to determine the monthly amount.

Do you have bills laying around that you need to open to get the amounts and determine due dates? If so, open them and include those items on the list that you are creating. There may be some items that are not due monthly. Maybe you pay them quarterly or even yearly. If they are paid quarterly, divide the amount that you pay by 3 and add that to the monthly list. If you pay them yearly, divide that number by 12 and add that to the list.

Now that you have this complete list, you should separate things into categories. There are many experts in this field. Each has their own system and technique used to move forward. Two of my favorites are Dave Ramsey and Tiffany Aliche, AKA, The Budgetnista. In her most recent book, "Get Good with Money", she outlines a very simple plan. The categories she describes are bills, variables, and cash. The bills are self-explanatory. These items come in the mail or via email monthly. The amount you pay is fixed and you will receive phone calls and letters if you miss a payment. Examples of these things are: mortgage, car note, and student loan installments.

The next category is variables. These are bills and/or necessary items and the amount that you pay every month changes based on how much is being used. Examples of this are: water, groceries, and electricity.

The last category is cash. Any item left that did not fit into the previous two categories goes here. After you have completed all three categories, add the sum of each. The number that you come up with is your current monthly expenses.

Next step is to write down all sources of income and total them. Compare your expenses with your monthly income. What does this show you? Are your bills more than income? You now have your baseline and know where you need to start. Congratulations!

Because I want to give the same amount of time to each chapter in this book, I won't go into great detail about next steps here. I could, however, because I am passionate about helping people to become financially aware, responsible, and free.

The basic thing that you need to know is that if your expenses are more than your income, you have three options. You can reduce expenses, increase income, or you can do a combination of both. Whichever you choose, know that there is no magic trick that will make things work out. Until these numbers match, your money will always be off balance and you will not get as far ahead as you could with a well-developed plan.

This basic step can be emotionally draining. Know that it is a means to an end, it is necessary, and you will get through it! This step requires you to ask yourself some very hard questions about what you want your life to look like. It will help you to identify your priorities. Being honest with yourself is extremely important here.

Breathe and Keep Going...

Once the day-to- day budget and financial matters are set, look at all the things for which you qualify. Are there insurance policies in place? Any work related benefits after a death? What about pension or IRA accounts that may need to be switched over to your name now that your loved one is gone? Eligible for social security?   Special funding? Scholarship/Grant? Pension? Workers' comp? Was the death related to some type of malpractice or some negligence that may require legal assistance? Leave no stone unturned. Even the smallest benefit may assist you and your family in the end. This part can be overwhelming especially if you are not in the finance/insurance/legal field and are familiar with terms, etc. Get help from professionals!

When you find out what you may qualify for, take your time to gather all the paperwork they are requesting to start the process. Make the appointments to submit paperwork where needed. Take care of securing one benefit at a time. Do not overwhelm yourself and only do what you can. Ask for help where needed. Maybe someone can watch the kids for you. Maybe someone can drive you around so you don't have to worry about finding a place to park. Perhaps someone can be there with you for moral support when you break down in the social security office as you explain the reason you are applying. Maybe someone can cook a meal for you on the day of one of your appointments so that you don't have to think about it for that day. It all helps.

ESTATE PLANNING

Here we are. You have assessed your current situation; you have developed a budget and are sticking to it. You have submitted all documents for anything that you and your family qualify for. Now it is time for you to look at or revisit planning for your future. Even if you have done this to some degree, it will look different now that your loved one is no longer a part of the plan. This again can be overwhelming. It is a necessary step, but take your time and do what you can.

I am going to provide a couple of definitions for terms that you may come across as you are researching and talking with an estate-planning specialist:

Executor/Personal representative: The person that you appoint who will divide all the money and assets that you have left after you are deceased.

Beneficiary: The person that you appoint who actually receives whatever it is that you assign to them.

Testator: The person who writes a will.

Will: The document that simply states how things are to be divided.

Pour over will: A very general will that states, "I leave everything to my trust." A will is a public document. Anyone can access the details of a will. This type of will prevents everyone from having the specific details of your record.

Trust: A private document that spells out very specific directives after you are gone.

Living Trust: A trust that was created during your lifetime

Living Will: Gives medical directives if you become incapacitated for some reason.

Power of attorney: A person appointed to make decisions and sign paperwork and will represent you in your absence if you cannot represent yourself. A "durable" power of attorney takes effect immediately. A "general" power of attorney takes place after you die.

I highly recommend that you do some basic research on this topic and then speak with a professional in this area. These three basic steps will help you as you develop the plan that is right for your family:

First, if you are a parent, you want to make a plan for your children if something were to happen to you. You are the only parent left and you don't want to leave this to chance. Ask yourself the simple question, "Who do I want to care for my children if I am no longer able to do so?" Depending on the size of your family and how simple the plan may be, you may be able to accomplish this with a simple visit to the office supply store or an online template.

Second, you want to make a plan for any things of value and assets that you have. Start this process by taking inventory of what you have. Make a list of valuable clothes, vehicles, real estate, jewelry, bank accounts. Then determine how you would want these to be divided. Would everything go to your children evenly? Would you bless someone with that fur coat that sits in your closet? Does each account that you own have a beneficiary assigned to it?

Lastly, you want a plan for any lump sums that would be coming, (i.e. insurance payouts). Who will you assign as beneficiary? Do you want any money divided equally among all children? Who do you want to assign to oversee that the instructions that you leave are carried out the way you want them? What about in the event that you are incapacitated and unable to make medical decisions? Do you have someone that you trust to do that for you?

I know that these things sound overwhelming but if you seek assistance from the right professional, they can easily hold your hand through this process. I have included some resources in the back of the book that you may find helpful.

Breathe and Keep Going…

Chapter 10

Spirituality

No matter what it is that you believe, death is one of those things that will put your ideology to the test. Even if you are one that has no formal belief system, death will raise questions. I suggest that you hold on to whatever serves and comforts you during this time. If your beliefs support you, keep you grounded, give you purpose and meaning, comfort you, clarify things for you, and maybe even provide some answers, carry on with them. Dig deeper into reading its doctrine and teachings. Read, listen to podcasts and speakers, and surround yourself with those who have the same beliefs as you. This will bring you some peace. If your current beliefs do not provide the above, it may be time to assess them to determine if they are still true for you.

Every ideology has teachings and thoughts about death, grief, and the afterlife. They often give some sort of guidance and guidelines of what to do when a tragedy occurs. Sit still and listen to your inner voice, your inner knowing. Trust yourself and your answers. Whether you believe that this insight comes from God, Spirit, Intuition, Allah, Jesus, Nature, Universe, a combination of some or all fore-mentioned, or somewhere else altogether, it doesn't matter one bit. You have it, just listen! Ask yourself the hard questions like:

- What is the meaning and purpose of life? Why? How do I know this to be true? Does this ideology serve me right now?

- What does it mean to live your life responsibly? Why? How do I know this to be true? Does this ideology serve me right now?

- What do I believe happens in death? Why? How do I know this to be true? Does this ideology serve me right now?

Questioning the foundation of each belief will assist you in realizing if it is something that is genuinely the way you feel, your own personal values, or something that was handed down to you from some other place; maybe even from generation to generation. You may be shocked at your answers. Although we are discussing this here in this chapter related to spirituality, this concept applies to all areas of life. Whether you "check in" with yourself in this manner every 5 years, yearly, quarterly, monthly, or daily, I encourage you to make it a regular practice.

These types of self-checkpoints are critical and necessary. We go through different things and learn different lessons along the way. Our experiences, relationships, and circumstances affect our outlook on life and definitely should have an impact on our thoughts and therefore our actions. Nobody stays the same. So why should everything in our lives? We must know where we are, our starting point, to know where we are going.

You may find yourself needing to let go of some things and adding others. This can be uncomfortable and scary. That however, does not mean it is the wrong thing to do. You will get through it! You can do hard things. All will be well. Trust that it is unfolding just the way it should. Let those old things that no longer serve you go. You are an adult. You are not wrong for what you believed previously. You are not wrong if it no longer serves you. You get to change your mind. You owe it to yourself to make decisions to do those things that are best for you. If not you, then who will? If not now, then when? Everything in your life needs to reflect who you are and where you want to be. This includes ideologies around people or food or habits or doctrine or whatever. Question it all.

What happens if you have no belief system at all? What if you have more questions than answers and have no "base" from which to pull or even assess if some particular system is working for you or not? Start with yourself. Ask yourself some of the same questions

73

mentioned above. What is important to you? How do you believe people should be treated? How do you believe that you should behave in certain situations? What about daily practices? Basic morals or codes that people should have?

Next, look around your circle. Who are the people that display these particular behaviors and have these attributes? Talk to them about their beliefs. Do they have a specific doctrine they follow? This may be a good place, at least to begin exploration to determine if it is something there for you as well. If not, you will have at least tried something and you have something from which to pull and compare. Maybe you like three components and can incorporate them into your life but you do not like two very specific things. Then do not use or do those things that don't serve you. This is your life and you get to create it just the way you want to. There is no cookie cutter way that works for all.

In order to reach a specific destination, you must first have a starting point. This starting point or foundation is what will be built upon layer by layer to get you where you need to be. Your current beliefs and value system is that foundation. Get clear on what those things are and you will be able to build from there.

Whether you are leaning into what you believe, changing the narrative completely, or beginning to explore this area for the first time in your life, remember to put your faith in the principles and not the people teaching it or sharing their experiences with you. If you do so, this will disappoint you every time. These people are just that, people, and they are imperfect. Eventually, one of them will say or do something that does not line up with whatever

74

doctrine they are sharing. This does not mean the doctrine is wrong. It just means that the people involved are humans.

Keep your eyes on what is important and keep moving forward. Every person that comes into our lives carries a lesson for us. Maybe they are a mirror for us and aggravate us to our core. Most of the time when this occurs, the things that aggravate us in that person, are the things that we do not like about ourselves and really want to change. Sit with that and do some work in that area.

Maybe they are supportive in a time of great need and are meant to be there until the need is decreased or totally eliminated. These are just a couple of examples. The point is to identify the lesson they bring, honor it, and keep moving forward.

Breathe, Drink Water, and Keep Reading...You got this!

Chapter 11

Our Seeds

For a lot, if not most of us, our children are our priority and they are in the forefront of our minds with most of our decisions. Death of a loved one is no different. I had the experience of dealing with children in each age group when my husband passed. I will share specific things that I noticed. It is important to note that the ages and behaviors listed for each group are approximate and may overlap. For instance, some professionals consider adolescents to be from age 10-19. They are 13-18 for purposes of this chapter. Hey, this is not a book on child development; it is about being a widow…give me a break! LOL

In general, children will not be the same. Don't expect them to be. They are grieving just like you are and this will look different depending on the gender, depending on their age, depending on their personality, depending on their maturity, just to name a few variables. I think that you get the point. No two children are alike. In fact, your child(ren) may be one way on Monday and wake up like a totally different person on Tuesday. It's all an ebb and flow.

Some may become very silent and withdrawn. Some may be temperamental, some may begin to be belligerent and fight. Some may become bookworms. Some may be an emotional wreck. Some may become promiscuous. The point is, grief comes in all forms. The parent simply needs to take note of what is happening with each child and give them the resources they need for each step, stay connected, show support, and above all show love. I use the word "simply" loosely in regards to what the parent needs to do. None of this is "simple". Take it slow. Take your time. Do what you can do. Seek help. You know your kids better than anyone else. Just keep an eye on them.

Something else to consider at this time is that YOU are going through the grieving process too. You may not notice differences in your children's behaviors and realize what is "out the norm". Ask for help! Grief changes our lens of life, our perspective. Things are just not seen the way they were prior to the significant loss. Our thoughts, problem solving, and processing are affected in a MAJOR way. Know this and know that this is normal. You may be aware enough to see that your child's grades are falling, but you may not see that they no longer speak to their best friend. You may get extremely frustrated at your toddler who was doing very well with potty training and may not realize that the reason you have to go back to square one with them is related to grief and the changes in their world. You may just be so consumed in your own grief that you miss cues that you would have picked up before the loss. It's normal. Give yourself grace.

Missing the mark in some areas is common. This is the reason that checks and balances are important. Ask a trusted person(s), that is familiar with your children's traits, to partner with you. Maybe they will notice things that you had not been able to see or even considered.

Here are a couple pointers that could be helpful no matter the age or gender of your child(ren):

Self-care is first. You cannot pour from an empty cup. You will have nothing to give if you don't get yourself together first. You have a life outside of them (especially for older kids). Don't lose sight of this and make all decisions based on what your child(ren) would want. You are the parent, remember that. And although some hate to think so, they won't be around forever. They will grow, move out, have families, jobs, lives of their own and time with you will decrease. If your entire existence is based around them, this will leave you stuck, lonely, and feeling lost when the transition occurs.

Be patient. Nothing will be "normal" again and don't expect it to be. Now let's take a look at each group specifically.

Infant (birth to 1 year) This age group is often overlooked with the grieving process because most feel that these children are too young to understand the concept of death. Although this is true to some extent, they can certainly notice changes to routine as well as sense the emotional differences with their caregivers and those around them. Changes in sleeping patterns, eating schedule, skin issues (i.e. rash/hives), dietary choices, fussiness, desire to be close to or held by a specific person(s), need to be in a certain place or even certain room may be some of the things that you notice that could be related to grief.

Be patient with them. If you notice any of these things and you are at a loss on how to assist, SEEK HELP! Ask someone who has gone through the process, ask someone who has children that have exhibited the same qualities, read a book, a blog, YouTube, whatever! Do not just throw your hands up and frustrate them or yourself any more than the current stressors are already doing. Other things that may assist are keeping routines the same, speaking calmly to them, providing comforting items (i.e. blankie, pacifier), holding and cuddling them more often. Know that the main thing that infants and toddlers need at this age is security. The lost loved one may have played a big part in that. It will take some adjusting and time for this to level out again. Believe me, it will.

Toddlers (1 year to 3 years old) Toddler years are a time when you see rapid growth in children's cognitive development, language, and motor skills. They go from crawling everywhere and babbling or making sounds as a way to communicate to walking then running/jumping and talking excessively.

Grief may affect this age group in some of the same ways mentioned in infants. However, this group may also exhibit: regression in potty training, delay or total regression in items listed above. Here too, be patient. Know that this is a possibility but speak to a professional if you have concerns. Do not dismiss any delays as a sign of grief. Better to be on the side of caution than miss an opportunity to assist. Other things that may assist are the same as with infants above: keeping routines the same, speaking calmly to them, providing comforting items (i.e. blankie, pacifier), holding and cuddling them more often.

Preschooler (2-5 years old) This is what I call the "free" age, they just want to be free. The sentence "I can do it myself" is heard at least 1000 times a day. Children are becoming independent and prepping to separate from their caregivers and go to school. They attempt to master skills like picking out their clothes, bathing themselves, getting dressed in the morning, and feeding themselves. Along with the things that we have already mentioned for other groups, parents may see their preschoolers: becoming "clingy", looking for the absent person, having dreams/nightmares, or becoming anxious or fretful.

Comforting them by showing physical affection (hugs, cuddling, kisses), words of encouragement, and keeping their routines as consistent as possible will help during this time. It may also be helpful to allow them to have something that belonged to the deceased parent (i.e. a piece of clothing, a hairbrush, pillowcase, framed photo, etc.) Many companies will transform articles of clothing into things like blankets, teddy bears, and quilts.

School aged (6-12 years old) This is the time these children try to find their place among peers. Their bodies are changing rapidly. Young girls are developing into young women and boys are developing into young men. These children are trying to find out where they belong and who they are. Losing a part of themselves, as they are trying to put other pieces together, is a big blow.

You may find that children in this age group are more likely to look for reasons to blame themselves for a parent's death. Some other common behaviors are: not wanting to attend school or other functions, feeling embarrassed and/or different from their peers, developing aggressive (or complete opposite withdrawing from everything) behaviors, complaining of physical ailments (i.e. stomach aches, headaches, etc.)

Along with things mentioned above for other age groups, allowing questions, conversations, and providing honest answers, cuddling and comforting by physical touch helps children through the grief process. If they don't want to be touched for a while, reassuring them that they are loved (actually telling them those words) and informing them that death is out of their control and is definitely not their fault, are all things that can help this age group.

Do not put them down or pressure them for wanting to talk too much or too little. Some parents find that their children want to talk about the loved one all the time and it may be a trigger and too much for the parent. You do not want to silence them but you also want to honor your feelings as well. Don't rush them through their feelings, be dismissive, or think that their grief is supposed to look a certain way. If talking about the deceased is too much for you, find someone that they can talk to and express themselves. Encourage expression through play and art if that is what they like and want to do.

Adolescent/Preteen/Teen (13-18 years old) This is the age when children are continuing to develop physically and they are also obtaining knowledge and skills about how to manage their emotions and relationships. This critical time is the bridge between childhood and adulthood. Adolescence is the hardest time, in my opinion, to deal with losing a parent, not to say that any age group is easy. Children are going through puberty (which is craziness and presents its own set of challenges) and trying to figure it all out.......ALL OF IT...... Where do I belong? Who are my friends? What is happening to my body? What makes me tick? Why am I sad one minute and happy the next?

Common things that may occur during this period include restlessness, inability to focus on things, blaming one's self for death, anxiety about other parent or even themselves dying, strained relationships, suicidal thoughts, and dreams/nightmares regarding death. Jokes or morbid sense of humor to mask pain/sadness, bedwetting, withdrawing from people/activities, or the opposite with wanting to be around family all the time.

To add grief on top of all the changes this age goes through, can seem almost unbearable to some. Seek Help! Recruit as many as you can to assist and make sure that you aren't missing the mark. Do regular "check ins" (as with all the groups) to make sure they are receiving what they need. This may change from month to month, week to week, day to day, or hour to hour. That is ok. Let the consistent thing be the fact that you are there supporting them and giving them what they need each time, every time.

The "help" does not always have to look the same way. Some major things that I have found are important for this group are:

Acknowledging their feelings around grief and the emotions that come with going through this process.

Having no expectations regarding their behaviors but rather gently supporting them through things. Do not expect them to "act like an adult" and carry on as normal.

Sharing your feelings and plans as their parent. They often feel like they are all alone or weak because we as parents want to shield them from our grief. For some reason we have been programmed to believe that we are supposed to present as superheroes and be almost robotic to our children. As if, we have no emotions. It's ok for them to see us cry. It's ok for them to see us stay in the bed all day occasionally. It is ok for us to discuss that we are sad and that we relate to them! Kids need consistency, love, and support from parents. Knowing that this is heartbreaking, earth shattering, and you will get through it together will do wonders!

Helping these children find their place, connecting them with people and things that "fit them" is the key to sanity for this group. What do they like? Do they want to connect with others their age who have suffered a loss? Trying different things may also be a key factor here. It's difficult to know what it is that you want if you haven't tried much. Explore with them. Be creative. Encourage them to brainstorm and then just do it!

Adults - As parents, we want to take care of all our children. That is natural. Our adult children are no different. However, the key word here is adult. We always have to be mindful of that. First, recognize where your adult child is and honor that. Is this a child that is still in your home and may need some extra care due to where they are emotionally, physically, socially, according to maturity level? We know that just because someone reaches a certain age that does not mean that they are ready to embrace the world as a full-grown, fully equipped, member of society. One size does not fit all here. For purposes of this section, I am speaking of those adult children that are fully functioning and self-supporting and either out of the home or on their way out.

Help these children where you can. Guide them in the right direction and encourage them to seek the needed resources. Again, allow them to do that. It is not your role to force them. Know that we have given them all of the resources that they need to handle what life throws their way. Our pain, anguish, insomnia, stress over their decisions does not help them, but does hurt us and may even delay our healing that needs to occur when we are overly involved with their issues. Check in with them but do not overpower or shadow or make them feel as if their grief has to look your way. You are only in control of your own behaviors and reactions, not theirs. You have self-care to do.

Deep breath…drink water…almost there…keep reading…

Chapter 12

Intimate Relationships

Disclaimer: I do not claim to be any type of relationship expert whatsoever. I will not tell you what is best for your circumstance after losing someone you love. To do so would be contrary to the theme of this entire book. This is YOUR journey! I hope that these tidbits of information will help you as you figure it all out.

Dating and having another intimate relationship may be the furthest thing from your mind right now. That's ok and absolutely nothing wrong with that. On the other hand, it may be all you can think about. There is absolutely nothing wrong with that either.

Maybe you are wondering about the type of eligible people that are out there in the world. Maybe you are wondering if anyone will find you attractive. And, maybe you are wondering if you even know how to date anymore. What if you are wondering if you even want to be in another relationship? Or, maybe your thoughts vacillate between all of the above.

If nobody else tells you, I personally want you to know that any and every place that your thoughts take you is totally fine. They are YOUR thoughts. They are valid. They are important. They are ok. Acknowledge and honor your feelings. Process them. Don't run from them. Do not bury them, push them aside, or act as if they don't exist.

IT'S DIFFERENT

Know that when and if you decide to enter into the dating world again, it will not be the same as when you were dating your deceased partner or spouse. This may sound like a simple concept and something that we should already know but it isn't.

If you have been with your partner for 10 years, (even a couple years) and have not experienced dating outside of that person, know that the experience will not be the same. People change, societal norms change, technology changes, etc. Know that different does not mean bad. The rules may change. The expectations may change. The way in which it is done may change. But, your morals, values, and desires do not have to change. Give yourself grace and time to learn what is new and different. Be patient. Find someone who is single that you trust and admire, and talk to them about what they do, what they avoid, and how they do it. Ask them if they will be your dating mentor/coach. Take it all in and spit out what is not for you. Tweak it as many times as necessary to make it your own.

Some of you may have the desire to jump back into a relationship, any relationship, so that you can feel "normal" again. I highly suggest you stay away from this urge. Oftentimes when the dust settles, there are more regrets than there could have been if you had just taken time out to continue processing and healing.

KNOW EXACTLY WHAT YOU WANT OR BE STILL UNTIL YOU DO

"The easiest way to navigate through all the changes is to have a firm foundation. The foundation is built on knowing what you want. Decisions are easy when values are clear."

~Unknown~

First, think about these things. What will make you happy? How does another person fit into your life at this time? When you visualize everything that a relationship entails, are you ready for all of it? Are you looking to simply date or looking for marriage? Long term courting? Just sex? If applicable, have you considered how or if this will affect your children, family, and friends? Your home? Your job? Your personal space?

Make your list of what you want and what you do not want. What are absolute deal breakers for you? Review this list often and revise as necessary. Stick with this list when you meet candidates and don't waste your time if it doesn't line up! Now, I am not saying make a list the length of your arm that details all the physical attributes of a person that you want as a mate and then you turn down the opportunity to get to know the person that meets all criteria except they have blue eyes instead of brown. (But, there is

89

nothing wrong with having a fluid list of what your preferences are either).

Instead, what I am speaking of avoiding is more like a situation where you are spending your time and energy with a person that you really like, knowing that they definitely want another child and you definitely do not. You will just be postponing the inevitable. This is a recipe for disaster and hurt. No one needs to be in a situation where they feel they are "settling." Be honest with yourself and others and require they do the same.

Our desires are energy. What we put out and visualize, pray about, verbalize, affirm, dream, spend money on, and give attention to is what we will attract to ourselves. It's worth it to take the time to: 1) Know what our true desires are, 2) Be aware of our current words, thoughts, and actions to determine if they are aligned with our desires. Be honest with yourself about this and the process. I know that I keep saying this sentence. I do so because it's extremely important! If you get nothing else out of this book, I hope that this is one point that you will hang onto. Cut out everything that does not line up with what you want. Your desires and dreams are important and they can and will come true.

Know that things are ever changing. As we grow and evolve, our desires and interests grow as well. There is nothing wrong with this and do not let others make you feel that it is. You can think you want one thing one day and something happens in your life that totally changes your perspective. That is ok too! It's ok to modify the list I spoke of above, even daily if needed.

Although it is perfectly ok to change your mind and revise what suits you as often as you see fit, you may want to consider that changing your mind too frequently could be a sign that you need to just sit still and take some more time to allow your vision to be clearer. Sitting still, in peace, is underrated and we definitely don't do it enough. Silence and stillness allows us to hear our inner voice clearly and avoids crucial mistakes.

WAYS TO DATE

There are various ways to meet people: word of mouth, blind dating, online dating, social media (i.e. Live Waves, Facebook, Instagram), old fashion going out ,whatever you choose, make sure it feels right to you. Do not rush. Take your time and don't be pressured by friends, family, to do anything that you are not ready for. That being said, there is a difference between a gentle nudge and a push. Try new things. It's totally fine to stick your toe in the water and pull it right back out if it's too cold.

CHILDREN

When it comes to dating, there are many things to consider and there are as many opinions as there are people in the world. As with all the sections in this book, I would simply say, take time to know what YOU want, consider everything; make the decisions that align with your desires.

As it relates to children, things you may want to consider are: age of the children, sex of the children, what type of relationship you would want this person to have with your children (if any), how much you will communicate with your children about the person, when and if you will introduce the person, just to name a few.

Know that you do not have to have all of this figured out before you accept a phone number from an interested party. It is, however, a good idea to consider these things along the way and not be blissfully ignorant about the impact they could have on your future.

Chapter 13

Stimulate your "Why"

You made it! You read each chapter. Or, maybe you didn't and you skipped all around the book and read what you thought was for you. Either way, you did something that can benefit you and your family, and I am proud of you. You can do hard things. You have done hard things. The road ahead may not be easy but know that you are capable, supported, and definitely are not alone!

It is my hope that you have found something interesting and helpful in the content of this book. I want to emphasize and reiterate that this is your journey and none of it has to look like anyone else's. Take your time. Be patient with yourself. Get the help you need for you and your family. Remember, drink your water, inhale, exhale, you got this. WE got this…

Resources & References

Finances
"Get Good with Money" by Tiffany Aliche aka The Budgetnista
https://thebudgetnista.com
"The Total Money Makeover" by Dave Ramsey
https://www.ramseysolutions.com
"The Complete Guide to Money" by Dave Ramsey

Support for Women
BeFree Inner Circle www.befreeproject.com

Support for writers/creators
Lynda D. Mallory www.lyndadmallory.com
Jeanette Brewster www.jeanettebrewster.com

Support for widows
Michele Neff Hernandez www.soaringspirits.org
Michelle Steinke-Baumgard www.onefitwidow.com

Spiritual Support
Sarah Jakes Roberts https://sarahjakesroberts.com
Joyce Meyer https://joycemeyer.org
Priscilla Shirer https://www.goingbeyond.com

Support through art
Evelyn Mann-Carter https://evelynmc.net
Sierra Casher www.sierracasher.com

Support for widows and families in fire service
National Fallen Firefighters Foundation https://www.firehero.org

Support with Mental health and substance abuse
SAMHSA's National Helpline www.samhsa.gov (referral service)
Better Help https://www.betterhelp.com (online counseling)

Self-care
Coffee subscription service www.caffeinatedjoy.com
Emotional awareness/healing www.positivelifehaven.com
Online fitness www.fitnesswithpj.com

Home cleaning/organization
Fly Lady www.flylady.net
The Minimal Mom www.theminimalmom.com

Yoga
Yoga with Adriene www.yogawithadriene.com

Favorite podcasts
The Heart of Chat www.theheartofchat.com
Woman Evolve www.womanevolve.com
Grief in Progress https://getpodcast.com/podcast/grief-in-progress

Printed in the USA
CPSIA information can be obtained
at www.ICGtesting.com
LVHW011339290923
759316LV00004B/8

9 780578 374765